Hightime You Made A Move!
A Motivational Book For Success

Jane John-Nwankwo

Copyright © 2014 Jane John-Nwankwo

www.janejohn-nwankwo.com

All rights reserved.

ISBN-13: 978-1497343573

ISBN-10: 1497343577

DEDICATION

Dedicated to all who wish to achieve

Have you purchased these books?

Table of Contents

1. **Why We Procrastinate**
   What is a Procrastinator?

   Procrastination Motivation

   The World of the Procrastinator

   How Does a Procrastinator become one?

   Characteristics of a Procrastinator

   Why is Procrastination Bad for You?

   Finding Solutions

2. **Decision Making**

   Life's Everyday Decisions

   Types of Decision Makers

   The Decision-Making Process

   Why it's Important to have a Decision-Making Strategy

   Decision-Making Tips

3. **Being Satisfied with Our Actions**

   Evaluating Our Choices

   A Call to Action

4. **Helpful Resources**

Have you bought these books?

HAVE YOU BOUGHT THESE BOOKS BY THE SAME AUTHOR?

1. Accept Challenges

2. Never Be Intimidated

3. Design Methods To Navigate

4. Success Is For The Ready

5. How to Make A Million in Nursing

6. Jokes for Nurses

Visit www.janejohn-nwankwo.com

This book is a motivational and inspirational book written to empower individuals of every age to achieve their life dreams. It is the first of the 5 books in the "It's in your hands" series. The 5 books in the series were spelt from the word: HANDS, because, it's in your HANDS to succeed!

H- Hightime you made a move!

A-Accept challenges

N- Never be intimidated

D- Design ways to navigate

S- Success is for the ready

Introduction

I stepped into a physical therapy clinic in an attempt to advertise one of my books "Nurses' Romance" by distributing free copies. I started distributing copies to the patients who were waiting for their turn. I stretched out a free copy to a man, and he gladly grabbed it and asked me for a copy of another book he saw in my hands "Jokes for Nurses", claiming his wife was a nurse. I gave him the extra copy. I continued my task of distributing copies. As I stretched out a copy to give to one woman, she looked at me without stretching her hands. From her face, I could read that she did not believe that the book was free, so she did not want to stretch her hands to grab a copy, only to be asked for money later. I gave her a respectful, but befitting comment that made her to take the book. How often do we prefer to remain in our comfort zones without making a move because we are so afraid of what the move could cost us.

I know many of my friends that would like to own a couple of businesses as I do, but are so afraid to make a move-a move like not asking for extra nursing shifts (overtime) , but using their days off to try starting a business gradually before going full time. One of them said "It is better to hang on to the one you are sure". Yes I do agree. I so much buy the old proverb "A bird in hand is worth two in the bush", but the proverb did not say " Never go for the one in the bush".

The best time to take an action toward a dream is yesterday.

1. Why We Procrastinate

"The way to get started is to quit talking and begin doing."

~Walt Disney

Who is a Procrastinator?

Simply put: a procrastinator is someone who puts off work.

Motivation to Procrastinate

Studies by Ferrari and others show that procrastinators are motivated by three main reasons:

- Arousal types actually enjoy the "bad boy" or "high stakes thrill" of that the last minute adrenalin rush.

- Avoiders lack self-confidence and/or fear failure. If they are successful, they are concerned that this raises expectations and puts them in danger of future failure. It's easier not to try so others won't expect anything.

- "Wafflers" are decision procrastinators. They are literally paralyzed by having to make a decision. If they don't make a decision they don't have the responsibility attached to that decision.

- Passive resistors. Consciously or unconsciously, some procrastinators are rebelling against a parent, an older sibling, or a spouse who is a "doer" or a "planner" and applies pressure to try to "fix" a procrastinator.

- Perfectionists: Procrastinators tend to be perfectionists. They avoid because they are insecure. They feel they must be perfect to please others. So they often put things off and then fret that they won't be loved unless what they do is perfect.

The World of the Procrastinator

> *"NEVER PUT OFF TILL TOMORROW WHAT MAY BE DONE DAY AFTER TOMORROW JUST AS WELL."*
>
> **~Mark Twain**

Procrastination is an almost certain way to ensure we don't succeed. There is no better way to throw a well-laid plan off the road to success.

We are all guilty at one time or another of procrastinating. I procrastinate over doing my school work—until it is few hours to the deadline. Yet, I am efficient about completing most other tasks. It's easier to put things off than it is to actually get to work on them. Why do we procrastinate even when it is something we want to achieve or know we need to do?

Procrastinators shoot themselves in the foot. They set up road blocks just by putting things off until it is too late to achieve success. Consciously or subconsciously, they make choices that hurt their performance. Consider what time of the year it is now, and think of something you have been desiring to achieve for the past 10 months, but have been putting it off. Can you believe it is ten months already?

Psychologists say that twenty percent of any group is made up of chronic procrastinators. For them, procrastination is a way of life. They are late to work or to school *because* of traffic. They don't pay their rent on time *because* they received their paycheck late. They're late arriving at church *because* they wanted to sleep late on a weekend.

They are always the last ones to hand in their reports *because* of computer problems. One parent joked that her son would be late for his own funeral.

Because of their procrastination, they miss out of getting tickets to a concert, dinner reservations, and tea times. Their gift cards are never redeemed and their email remains unanswered. Chronic procrastinators are the ones who go Christmas shopping on Christmas Eve, buy the Thanksgiving turkey the morning it is to be cooked, and pick up flowers for their mother from a roadside vendor on Mother's Day morning.

In some societies, like Japan and China, procrastination is viewed as a major character flaw and an embarrassment to the family. In North America we see it as a personality quirk. That's why stores in North America stay open until midnight on Christmas Eve, stores carry unfrozen turkeys, and those roadside flower vendors do so well.

We're too tolerant of procrastinators to lecture them!

Those who try to "fix" a procrastinator start by trying to build time management skills. Procrastination is not a problem of lack of time management. Nor is it the result of poor planning. Procrastinators do not lack the ability to estimate time how much time things will take to get done. Procrastinators are not unaware of the passage of time. Nor are procrastinators busier than the rest of us.

Dr. Ferrari, once said, "Telling someone who procrastinates to buy a weekly planner is like telling someone with chronic depression to just cheer up."

How Does a Procrastinator become one?

HOW SOON 'NOT NOW' BECOMES 'NEVER.'"

~**Martin Luther**

Contrary to some theories, procrastinators are not born that way. Procrastination is a learned behavior. Often a procrastinator has one or two authoritarian parents who have made a career out of nagging and punishing tardiness.

When a parent is severe or controlling, children don't learn to self-regulate. They are never given the chance.

Sometimes procrastinating is a way to rebel against authority. It is a form of passive resistance.

Characteristics of Procrastinators

Hundreds of studies have been done on procrastinators trying to describe their character traits. The following five seem to be the most prevalent, appearing in most studies:

"Don't worry! I'll get around to it."

> When it comes to boring or distasteful tasks, procrastinators can be counted on to

say, "We've got lots of time before that's due!" When combined with forgetfulness, this can be a lethal combination. The batteries in the smoke alarm don't get changed. The safety gate doesn't get installed on the stairs. Income taxes don't get filed, traffic tickets don't get paid. The lint doesn't get cleaned out of the dryer. The heating bill wasn't paid. The gas gauge reads empty. You get the picture!

"It's no fun!"

Of course reading that new novel is more fun than logging on the internet to pay your TV bill. Of course playing that new computer game is more fun than doing homework. Of course going shopping at the mall is more fun than cleaning the house. Procrastinators don't do the boring tasks to get them out of the way. A chronic procrastinator will put off doing something in favor of even a slightly more interesting task. For Rather than clean the bathroom, he'll opt to wash the car. She'll dust ahead of paying the bills. Your son will load the dishwasher or take out the garbage to avoid doing homework.

"I work better under pressure!"

Some procrastinators have convinced themselves that putting a boring or distasteful job makes it less boring or distasteful because of the pressure to get it done on time. Others claim the stress of a short timeline improves their focus. Improved focus due to a tight timeline and higher quality of work under stress have never been scientifically proven. But procrastinators still cling to this myth.

"I can't hear you!"

Procrastinators are masters of ignoring a problem. They can block out the important but boring things like: homework, an essay, the garbage, etc. Procrastinators can remain completely oblivious to stressful problems until things climax or explode. They simply tune things and people out!

"Give me a moment."

If you ever need to stall, call on a procrastinator. Procrastinators can stall a situation. The stalling behavior becomes evident when a procrastinator meets a planner. As a matter of fact, if a procrastinator just did the task when it first comes up he would have used half as much energy as he did on planning evasions! But, procrastinators don't see it that way!

Why is Procrastination Bad for You?

We can all list the reasons why procrastination is bad for the rest of us. But why is it bad for the procrastinator?

- While procrastinators avoid and stall, delay only serves to increase life's stress. Some health studies involving college students have shown that procrastination can cause health problems like: of compromised immune systems, more colds and flu, and gastrointestinal problems and insomnia.

- Procrastination is closely linked to other unhealthy habits like lethargy, sloth, poor hygiene, lack of exercise, substance abuse, and obesity.

- Procrastination and poor quality work are closely aligned. Hasty, last-minute products—in spite of procrastinators' protests—are not higher quality work!

- Missed deadlines translate to lack of promotions, poor performance reviews, failed grades, not going back to school, not getting a first degree, not getting a masters, not passing a professional exam, not devoting time for family, rushing one's prayers, not having time even for oneself!

- No one likes to be used. If you procrastinate and beg for more time, it puts the other person in an uncomfortable position and others who did their work on time resent it. Procrastination is bad for social and work relationships. Procrastination has a high cost to others who have to take up the slack at home or work. Others become resentful. Procrastination destroys teamwork in the workplace and personal relationships

- Once developed, procrastination becomes a hard habit to break.

- Procrastination sends a bad message. Procrastinators let others down. Promises get broken and people expect less and think less of a procrastinator. They view procrastination like other crutches: alcohol, drugs, gambling…

- Procrastination is not seen as a positive trait when you are applying for a job, trying to get into a good college, or starting a business, or proposing to that dream partner.

- Procrastinators deceive themselves and others. Consequently people—including themselves—lose faith in the procrastinator's word.

- Procrastinators lack focus. They are so busy avoiding the task they know they should be doing that they all over the map avoiding the task.

- Procrastinators lose self-confidence and fear trying. They have spent so much time and energy NOT doing something that they fear attempting it.

Finding Solutions

While we can agree that a parent, teacher, sibling, colleague, or partner trying to "fix" a procrastinator is not the answer most procrastinators will admit that they really don't want to procrastinate or take pleasure in frustrating others with their behavior. Procrastinators have to be willing to admit that procrastinating behaviors are getting in the way of achieving what they want and deserve to have. Then, and only then, can procrastinators change their behavior.

Here are some tips from recovering procrastinators who have taken the first steps toward achieving their goals:

1.   Analyze the task. Break it into consumable sub-tasks.

> You know the old story: How do you eat an elephant? One forkful at a time. Well that's how to deal with a task that seems overwhelming. Break it down into manageable parts. Then deal with each part as a single entity. Soon, your task will be so simple that you won't believe you procrastinated at it.

2.   Alter your surroundings.

> Different environments affect productivity. If working from the desk or bed in your room lulls you to inactivity try the kitchen table. If the living room offers too many distractions, try the library. My friend who had four roommates completed his thesis on the fire escape. Another stayed at the office after work. I prefer to write my books

on my laptop, on my bed, where there are less distractions. There is always a better environment if you need to bump yourself out of a comfort zone.

3. Create a master plan

Sometimes just getting everything down in black and white with clearly defined deadlines is all the motivation you need.

4. Find out what nurtures your procrastination and eliminate it.

Identify what you do to distract yourself from what you should be doing and make it less accessible. Disable the automatic notification option in your email program. Leave your smart phone turned off. Don't stock the fridge with goodies. Get rid of the distractions. Log out of your email to avoid distractions.

5. Associate with people who have the traits you'd like to possess.

Choose to form relationships with people we have a positive influence on your behaviors. Identify the people/friends/colleagues/relatives that energize you and bring out the best in you.

6. Take a page from AA

Alcoholics Anonymous has taught us the importance of having someone to turn to when we feel we are sliding away from where we want to go with our goals. Choose someone with his/her own set of goals. Hold each other accountable to your goals and plans. While it's not necessary for both of you to have the same goals, it'll be even better if that's the case! Then you can learn from each other. It's always good to be accountable.

7. Verbalize your goals.

Tell others about your goals. Listen to what they sound like. Do they sound good? Does that goal roll pleasingly off your tongue? How do you feel when you say it? What are people's reactions?

Often our goals play around in our heads like fantasies. Once we actually say them out loud, things change. We've made a commitment to our goals, ourselves. Those goals become tangible. People don't laugh. Instead they ask how things are coming along. They may even offer resources or support. It's also a great way to keep yourself accountable to your plans.

8. Find a Mentor

Seek out someone who has already achieved what you hope to accomplish.

Seeing actual proof that your goals are very achievable if you take action is one of the best inspirations for action. "If he can do it, I can too."

9. Restate your dreams.

If you have been procrastinating for a long time over starting that dream business or finally writing that novel or going back to school to achieve your dream career, you might want to restate or "fine tune" your outcome. What exactly do you want to achieve? What should you do to get there? What are the steps to take? Does your current situation align with that? If it doesn't, what can you do about it? The goal of this book is to impact your life. Even if you are not a chronic procrastinator, you will be honest to say that you procrastinate returning phone calls, or simple things. Whenever you are tempted to procrastinate again, remember that It's HIGHTIME YOU MADE A MOVE!

10. Face reality and stop hiding behind excuses.

Are you waiting for a perfect time to go back to school or to get started on that novel or to start your own business? There will never be a perfect time! You will always be able to find excuses to hide behind. Ditch those excuses. If you keep waiting for one, you are never going to achieve that dream!

11. Get organized. Create a roadmap to success.

One way to commit to that first step in reaching your dream is to create a game plan. Write a detailed timeline. Include specific deadlines. If all you have is an end-goal, that's like handing a procrastinator a "procrastinate forever" card. Having no set dates for steps along the path to the gold at the end of the rainbow almost assures you will never arrive at that pot of gold. Creating a master timeline with specific tasks along the path is a roadmap to success. As you reach each task and check it off, it empowers you to continue. What you've done is create an urgency to act. Goals can be broken down into monthly, weekly, and even daily task lists. That list is a call to action. You must accomplish this by the specified date. Otherwise, your goals will be delayed or jeopardized.

2. Decision Making

Life's Everyday Decisions

- Chocolate or strawberry?

- Scrabble or Life?

- The red dress or the blue one?

- *The Catcher in the Rye* or *Doctor Zhivago*?

- Heads or tails?

- Truth or dare?

- The blue rattle or the yellow one?

Every single day of our lives, we make tons of quick decisions. Sometimes we even make them automatically or unconsciously. Sometimes, we agonize over them. We choose actions and form opinions and make decisions and arrive at conclusions in a complicated mental process influenced by our experiences, biases, reasoning, emotions, and memories. Some decisions are made of our own free will. Others are influenced by the expectations of others and what we believe is in our best interest or the interest of others.

Types of Decision Makers

In his book, *The Paradox of Choice*, author Barry Schwartz identifies two types of decision makers. He calls them satisficers and maximizers. Satisficers make a decision or take action as soon as their criteria are met. How high or low their criteria is not an issue. The criteria may be very low or high. Once the decision is made, they are satisfied. They've done their job.

Maximizers are obsessed with a desire to make the best decision. Even if something meets their criteria, they can't make a decision until they've examined every possible choice. Maximizers take years to buy a car, a house, new furniture...because they must read all the available information, check out every option, digest what they have learned and decide on the best dress, the best college, the most attractive pair of shoes, or most efficient coffee maker available.

Not surprisingly, satisficers are on the whole happier people than maximizers. Maximizers expend a lot of time and energy arriving at a decision. Then they stress about whether it was, indeed, the right decision.

The Decision-Making Process

A simple five-step decision-making process can be applied to every decision: personal, domestic, or business. By using this process we can reach a decision in an organized manner, confident that we had a plan.

Step One: Identify the decision.

> Sometimes the decision to be made will have been presented to the decision maker. Sometimes the decision maker has to define the option or clarify exactly what the decision entails. For example if you are choosing a college, programs offered, cost of tuition, accommodations, transportation would all figure into that decision.

Step Two: Explore all the possible options.

The next step requires the decision maker to research and investigate exactly what the alternatives are. This is where the maximizers take forever. Let's say you have decided to buy a bicycle.

Step Three: Gather information.

The decision maker collects or processes information that will be used to help guide the decision. Having collected and collated information the decision maker will then apply it to his criteria. Part of the information-gathering process might involve talking to experts, taking tours, reading, hands-on demonstrations, road tests…The data collected will then be studied and understood by the decision maker. The more important and/or life-changing the decision is, the more thorough the information-gathering process will be. Maximizers will spend months or years on this step.

Step Four: Arrive at a decision.

After information has been gathered and compared to criteria, a decision based on the data and the criteria is reached. Satisficers would list criteria: options, cost, track record, guarantee and shop until they found a bike that met their criteria. They would make their decision efficiently and be happy with it. Maximizers would amass a long list of complicated criteria—on a grid or spreadsheet, read about every brand, look in every store, compare, make a decision and then agonize over whether it was the wisest decision—or ultimately conclude that no brand met all their criteria and decide to delay purchasing the bike.

Step Five: Evaluate the decision.

The final step is to determine whether the decision was appropriate. This can be done by revisiting the criteria, deciding how happy you are with the decision, considering the outcomes of that decision.

Why it is Important to have Decision-Making Strategies

> *"YOU CAN'T MAKE DECISIONS BASED ON FEAR AND THE POSSIBILITY `OF WHAT MIGHT HAPPEN."*
>
> ~Michelle Obama

From the moment you awaken until the last thing before you nod off to sleep you are faced with decision-making every single day of your life. Some decisions warrant no more thought than a flip of the coin. Others require research and use of a decision-making process. An important skill is knowing when and how much information gathering and data processing to do.

In most decision-making scenarios, we follow a certain strategy or series of strategies to arrive at a sound decision. Some of the complex and life-changing decisions require a lot of time, research, effort, and mental energy before you take action. Just because it is hightime you made a move, it doesn't mean that action doesn't require a well-thought-out decision or series of decisions first! Don't confuse making a move with leaping before you think!

Here are some decision-making strategies that you might use. The most appropriate one will depend on the type of decision, your investment in it, and your personal decision-making style.

1. Single Facet

> Your decision hinges on a one feature. There are two choices: to buy or not to buy;

decaf or regular; least expensive; red or blue; heads or tails; yes or no. In a single facet strategy you block out other variables and focus on one feature only. So, for example, if your choice is black tie or business formal, you are eliminating other attire like sporty; preppy; business casual....If you are buying soap and your criteria is least expensive, you are eliminating things like scent, effectiveness, aesthetically pleasing, and most familiar brand.

The single-facet strategy is effective in call-to-action situations where the decision is pretty simple, you don't have much vested interest, and you don't want to waste time. This is not a good strategy for dealing with life-changing decisions.

2. The Additive Strategy

The additive method requires that you consider all the important features of each choice. Then you evaluate each option. This strategy is practical for an important decision and ridiculously time consuming for decision of lesser importance. The additive strategy is effective for selecting a college, a wedding venue, an expensive camera. It is ridiculous for choosing a brand of chewing gum or a bottle of wine to serve with dinner.

First you create a list of important features that you want in, say, a new car. Next you rate each possible option on a scale of -5 to +5. Important features like safety rating, all-wheel drive, ease of getting in and out of it might each get a +5 rating. Things like color, interior material, trunk size might rate a -5 rating. After you have looked at each option you simply tally your totals.

The additive strategy can be a great way to determine the best option among a multitude of choices. It can be very time consuming. This kind of time is warranted in making a life-changing decision. Many find the -5 to +5 scale comforting. For others it is limiting.

3. Eliminate by Aspects Strategy

This strategy, proposed by psychologist Amos Tversky in 1972, involved evaluating each option one characteristic with whatever feature you believe is the most important. If a choice doesn't meet that criteria it is eliminated. Your list of possible decisions gets smaller and smaller as you cross items off the list until you eventually arrive at just one decision.

4. Decisions-Making in the Face of Uncertainty

The first three strategies are effective in cut-and-dried decisions like buying a coffee maker or choosing a health club. However, when risks are higher—like quitting your job and starting you own business—there are some risks, ambiguity, or uncertainties involved. For example, imagine that you are running late for an important meeting. Should you drive above the speed limit in order to get there on time, but risk getting a speeding ticket? Or should you drive the speed limit, risk being late, and possibly losing a valuable contract? In this case, you have to weigh the possibility that you might be late for your appointment against the probability that you will get a speeding ticket. A decision like this involves risk and uncertainty. You are on the horns of a dilemma!

5. Weigh the Odds Strategy

Using past experience is sometimes an effective strategy. For example let's take that speeding versus missing an important meeting scenario. You might use past experience to decide whether to speed. Think of how many times you have seen people getting pulled over by a police officer on that particular road. If you cannot immediately think of any examples, you might decide to go ahead and take a chance. Weighing the odds has led to conclude that few people get pulled over for speeding on that route. If, however, you can think of numerous examples of people getting pulled over, you might decide speeding isn't worth the risk.

6. The Prototype Strategy

When trying to determine whether to

speed or not, you might think about whom is most likely to get a speeding ticket on that road: a teenage driver, a young girl in a flashy car, a senior citizen or a middle-aged businessman? If you don't fit the prototype then you may conclude the probability of getting that speeding ticket is quite low. The same holds true for people quitting their jobs to start a new business. This strategy can be as simple as reflecting on past experience or as complex as applying the five-step decision-making process to the question.

The strategy we use depends on various factors: time, cost, personal decision-making style, complexity of the decision, degree of ambiguity involved, how vested you are in the outcome.

Decision-Making Tips

1. Gathering more information takes time, energy, and may involve cost. Set your criteria first. Then collect sufficient information to make a logical decision. Decide in advance how much you need to know to make a choice of: tablets, colleges, restaurants, apparel. Make the choice and move on. Satisficers are much better at this.

2. Although decision making is a logical, scientific process, there comes a time when, armed with all the facts, and applying all the criteria, you just have to trust your gut.

3. Know when it is important to collect more information before making a decision. Often we can trust our expert intuition, based on previous experiences, when making choices about familiar problems. But when a decision is not within your area

of expertise, don't be too quick to jump to conclusions. This is where the maximizers shine!

4. Don't be afraid to seek help...but choose your sources. Psychologist Daniel Gilbert, who wrote *Stumbling on Happiness*, states that we do not always make very rational decisions. We are also not always very good at deciding what will most likely make us happy. He contends that it is a good strategy, if we don't have the knowledge or experience to make an informed decision, to ask someone else.

5. The media and manufacturers try to convince us that every decision we make is life-changing: toothpaste, biscuits, yogurt, feminine products...Keep things in perspective. Don't obsess over a decision about laundry detergent. It is not life threatening. Make a choice and move on!

3. Being Satisfied with Our Decisions

> *When it is obvious that goals cannot be reached, don't adjust the goals, adjust the action steps.*
>
> **~Confucius**

No matter whom you are or where you live, you are called to action or make a move each and every day. Whether you decide to act is in itself a decision AND YOUR VERY OWN DECISION; not your spouse's, not your parents', not your siblings'', not your children's. Your actions might involve something as safe as choosing which of Baskin Robbins 31 ice cream flavors to choose or as life-altering as whether or not to get married to him or her. That sounds like a great thing. But the goal of this book is to spur you into taking a bold step in your life.

Research has shown that the ever-increasing number of options for the choices we have to make don't make us happier. Consider for example: the telephone. Not so long ago the choice was: Do you want to have a telephone installed in your home or not. Now we are faced with a dizzying array of cell phone options and service plans. Such a number of features and the speed at which new ones are being offered often results in our being paralyzed with indecision.

Barry Schwartz, author of six books about human behavior, notes that students are graduating with a wide range and number of skills and interests. Rather than making their job selection choices easier, they are overwhelmed when it comes to choosing a career. Maximizers study every decision with painstaking detail. Then they reach an action plan based on careful, logical, exhaustive decision making. Satisficers look at the problem, select criteria, investigate and reach an action plan. Their process is often less systematic, less logical, more intuitive. Satisficers are, generally, happier with their action plan and more confident that it will work.

Maximizers see a world of endless possibilities and missed opportunities as soon as they select one option. Maximizers most often end up with the better paying job, better working conditions, more room for advancement than satisficers. But, the latter are happier with their lot. Once they have made a decision they cease to obsess over what might have been.

> ...THE GOAL OF THIS BOOK IS TO SPUR YOU INTO TAKING A BOLD STEP IN YOUR LIFE.

Why do maximizers feel less satisfied and less confident in their action plan? Their world is filled with possibilities unselected and opportunities untried. They are acutely aware of the physical and psychological cost of having been forced to choose. They look at all the options they had to reject to pursue just one career.

Is it better to be a satisfied satisficer or a monied maximizer? Is there a happy medium? It is a fact that some people will never be satisfied with the course of action they selected. Trying to maximize on every call to action will drive many people to distraction. Others will never be completely sure they have made the right choices because they considered so many options.

Lower expectations, few options considered may result in fewer regrets and greater satisfaction. Considering every option is necessary only on life's most important life decisions.

One action plan is not to act. This is a decision. It is

often made when there is insufficient data or the consequences of taking action are just too overwhelming, scary, uncomfortable and/or life-threatening for you to even consider. Perhaps the time just isn't right. Maybe others whose life will be affected by your decision deserve to be involved. Tony Robins says regarding inaction: "The real decision is measured by the fact that you've taken a new action. If there's no action, you haven't truly decided."

> *"ACTION IS THE FOUNDATIONAL KEY TO ALL SUCCESS."*
>
> ~Pablo Picasso

Evaluating Our Choices

Plous (1993) points out that the decisions we make and the actions we take rest on the way we see ourselves and interpret the world. Our decisions are influenced by our perceptions, our biases, our previous experiences,

and our personalities.

Action for the sake of action is as dangerous as a crippling fear to take action. We are filled with anxiety:

- How do we pick our choices over some alternatives?
- How can we predict the consequences of our choices?
- How will know when it is the 'right' choice for us?

> *"I KNOW THAT I HAVE THE ABILITY TO ACHIEVE THE OBJECT OF MY DEFINITE PURPOSE IN LIFE, THEREFORE, I DEMAND OF MYSELF PERSISTENT, CONTINUOUS ACTION TOWARD ITS ATTAINMENT, AND I HERE AND NOW PROMISE TO RENDER SUCH ACTION."*
>
> ~Napoleon Hill

A Call to Action

Everyone has

experienced an entrepreneurial moment or two. A great idea popped into your head. If carried out, if acted upon, that idea might well have improved the quality of humankind. It might have eased suffering, found a cure for a life-threatening disease. Your idea might have made your own life easier, more enjoyable, more meaningful.

Unfortunately a great idea on paper won't do anything for anybody. Action must be taken to get that concept off the page and into people's lives! That great idea sitting around in your head is probably doing more harm than good. It's like procrastinating. Work that you keep postponing results in stress, anxiety, fear, and even physical ill health.

We can all come up with a million excuses not to act:

>-My family needs my salary. I can't quit my job.
>-I'm on an upward career track. Now is not a good time
>-I haven't the capital to get the idea off the ground.
>-Maybe it just seems like a good idea.
>-If this idea is so great, how come somebody hasn't already implemented it?
>-My friends would think I was crazy.
>-My kids need my spare time. I can't afford to take the time now.
>-I don't know the first thing about running a business.

Henry Ford said, "Whether you think you can or think you can't, either way you're right" If you have a desire to make your dream a reality, you owe it to yourself to act. When? NOW IS THE TIME TO MAKE A MOVE! If you wait for the ideal time, it will never come. You will always have a long list of excuses why it isn't the right time. Great thinkers, great inventors, world leaders did not wait for the right time. Just do it. You know you can! If you believe in God, pray. Prayer gives you the inner peace and strength to take action knowing that God will make everything right.

Hightime you made a move!

4. Helpful Resources

Allen, David. (2002) *Getting Things Done.*

Covey, Steven. (2004) *The 7 Habits of Highly Effective People.*

Dwyer, Wayne. (2014). *I Can See Clearly Now.*

Hill, Napoleon. (1936) *Think and Grow Rich.*

Goulston, Mark. (1996) *Get Out of Your Own Way: Overcoming Self-Defeating Behavior.*

Harvey, Jason.(2010) *Achieve Anything in Just One Year: Be Inspired Daily to Live Your Dreams and Accomplish Your Goals.*

Mandilo, Og. (1968) *The Greatest Salesman in the World.*

Murphy, Joseph. (2008) *The Power of Your Subconscious Mind.*

Pink, Daniel. (2010) *Drive: The Surprising Truth about what Motivates Us.*

Robbins, Tony. (1991) *Awaken the Giant Within.*

Vincent Peale, Norman. (1952) *The Power of Positive Thinking.*

Ziglar, Zig. (2002) *How to Stay Motivated:*

Developing the Qualities of Success.

Hightime you made a move!

ABOUT THE AUTHOR

Jane John-Nwankwo CPT, RN, MSN, PHN is a motivational speaker and published author of more than 30 books which include textbooks for healthcare training, fiction for entertainment, and motivational books.
Simply search
"Books by Jane John-Nwankwo"
On Amazon.com

Visit her website:
www.janejohn-nwankwo.com

Have you bought this book?

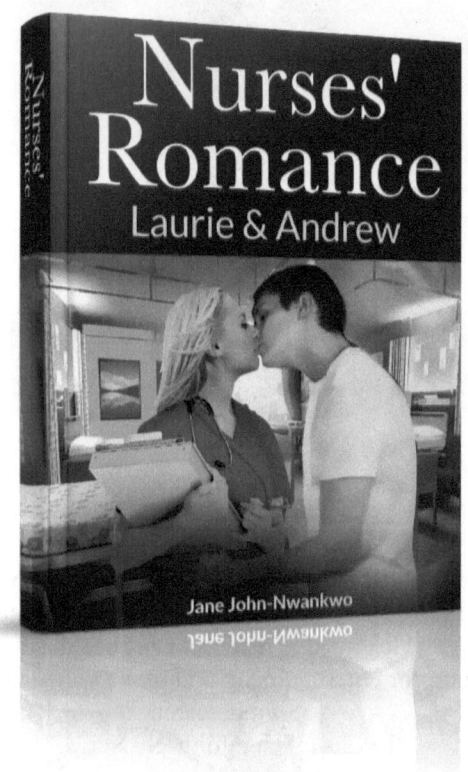

Hightime you made a move!

Visit www.janejohn-nwankwo.com

Have you purchased these books?

www.ingramcontent.com/pod-product-compliance
Lightning Source LLC
Chambersburg PA
CBHW021026180526
45163CB00005B/2135